The Bug Out Bag: What You Need to Stay Alive

by M. T. Anderson

Cover image courtesy of © Can Stock Photo Inc. / davisales

Dedication:

This book is dedicated to my dad, who instilled in me the belief one should always be prepared. I love you dad and miss you every day of my life.

Contents

The Bug Out Bag

If there's an item that can single-handed ensure your survival in the event of an emergency, it's the bug out bag. Regardless of whether you're forced to stay in your home, evacuate to the roof of your house or have to head for the hills, you're going to want to have at least one **bug out bag (BOB)** with you.

A bug out bag is a kit containing supplies that will be essential to your survival if you're cut off from all other resources. Your bug out bag should contain the supplies you need to last for at least 3 days. You can pack supplies for longer than that if you'd like, but keep in mind your focus should be on evacuation. 3 days is the minimum survival time you should shoot for.

The term "bug out" is used by those in the survival community to indicate a situation in which you need to get out of dodge in a hurry. The bug out bag is designed with this sort of scenario in mind. Its intent is to get you out of harm's way and to a safe location.

While bug out bags are designed to help you escape a bad situation, they can also be useful if you have to shelter in place. Sometimes natural disasters can strike unexpectedly and with such force you aren't able to get out of their path. You could end up stranded with no utilities in a very hostile environment. If you have a bug out bag handy, you'll have at least 3 days of supplies along with the ability to protect your supplies. Add in the food and water you already have in the house and you'll be in pretty good shape.

You can buy a bag that's already been made that purports to have everything you'll need to survive. The problem with going that route is you're buying a bag that's someone else's idea of the perfect bag. It may contain some of the items you need to survive, but it isn't going to contain all of the items you personally need or want.

I've seen these bags selling for as much as $2,000 per bag on the Internet. Sure, they contain top-notch gear, but how many of us really have $2K to put out on a bug out bag? My wife tolerates my survival awareness, but I don't think she'd be very tolerant of me draining our bank accounts on survival gear.

The good news is you can build your own bag for a fraction of the cost of an expensive prepackaged bag—with the added bonus that the bag you build will be tailored to your individual needs.

When I first started building my bag, I was inclined to throw in everything I could fit into it and call it a day. I squeezed all kinds of survival tools into every nook and cranny. I packed a bunch of food, water and extra clothes just in case. I thought I had the perfect bag—until I tried it on. It was so heavy I could barely get out of the house wearing it, let alone hike off into the wilderness with it weighing me down.

You have to carefully select your items based on the needs of your needs and the needs of those who are traveling with you. Your bag will grow (or shrink) and change as your needs change. A bag for a family with a baby is going to look a lot different than a bag for a single man, which is going to look a lot different than a bag for a family of three with no small children.

A good bug out bag is a work of art. The weight of each item has to be weighed against its usefulness and you have to be willing to sacrifice comfort for utility.

This book provides you the information you need to build your own bug out bag(s). While one bag is good, you eventually should shoot for a bug out bag for each member of your family that's capable of carrying one. The more supplies you're able to pack with you, the better off you'll be. At a bare minimum, you need one bag. Once you've got one complete, you can start on bags for everyone else. You are planning on taking them with you, aren't you?

Choosing the Best Bug Out Bag

Figure 1: The size of your bag is going to depend on the location you're bugging out to.

The best bug out bag is the one that's going to get you to your destination intact. It should be big enough to hold everything you need it to hold and durable enough to withstand a bit of abuse. You can't predict the situation you're going to be running from and you can't say for sure where you're going to end up, so it's best to have a bag that's able to take a beating.

I've seen people who keep their supplies in paper and plastic bags. I've also seen supplies stored in plastic totes with lids. I've even seen an entire bug out kit stored in a suitcase. It's also common for people to have a lot of the gear they'll need to survive, but it's spread out all over the house or stacked in a far corner of the attic. None of these storage solutions are a good idea.

Here's why.

Say you're sitting at home and there's a loud knock at the door. You answer the door and are told your neighborhood is being evacuated and you have 10 minutes to grab your gear and go. If you have to grab multiple items from various areas of your house, you're going to be in trouble. You'll be running around like a chicken with its head cut off trying to gather everything you need.

You're taking an already stressful situation and making it even more stressful. The more pressed for time you are, the more likely it becomes that you'll forget something. When it comes to survival gear, a single forgotten item can mean the difference between making it to your destination and not making it at all.

Keeping your supplies in bins, bags or a suitcase in a single location in your house means you'll be able to grab them and get them out to your vehicles if the need ever arises. You're a step ahead of the person searching his garage for his tent stakes. Where all 3 of these items fail is in their portability.

What happens if you have to abandon your vehicle and set off on foot? You aren't going to be able to carry bins, a bunch of bags or a suitcase off into the wilderness, especially if there's somebody hot on your trail. You're going to end up having to leave a lot of your gear behind if you have to leave your vehicle.

Even a duffel bag isn't ideal in this situation. Have you ever tried carrying a fully loaded duffel bag around for hours? I haven't either, but I know when I played baseball, I used a duffel bag for my gear and it started cutting into my hands even on short hikes to the field. I can't imagine what it would feel like after hiking a whole day carrying one.

Your bug out bag needs to be some sort of backpack that you can carry on your back to spread out the weight of the load.

A day back or kid's school backpack isn't going to cut it, unless you plan on surviving on the bare minimum required to survive. Sure, they're lightweight, but they aren't big enough to hold everything you're going to need.

A camping backpack that's capable of bearing a heavy load is a good choice. You have two general types of camping backpack to choose from: those with internal frames and those with external frames. There are also hybrid frame bags that are a combination of internal and external.

An internal frame bag has a frame contained inside the bag. The bag and frame come as one piece with the frame sewn inside the fabric of the bag. An external frame bag has frame on the outside. It's usually attached to the bag via a number of pins or clasps. Internal frame bags are good in that the frame is hidden away and the bag is less likely to get caught up on branches if you're pushing your way through heavy brush. The tradeoff is you don't have as many places to hang gear from as you do with an external frame. In the end, it boils down to personal preference. Get the bag you feel most comfortable with.

The size of bag you need depends on a number of factors. People living in colder climates are going to need bigger bags because they'll need bulky cold-weather gear to survive. If you live in a mild climate, you can probably get away with a smaller, lighter bag.

You'll also need to consider the availability of water. If you're headed into the mountains, there will probably be water close at hand. You can pack a small canteen or jug full of water and a purification device and you'll be good to go. You won't need to carry a large amount of water, so you can use a smaller bag than a person who has to bring three gallons of water to survive a 3-day trek through the desert.

Another consideration you need to make is the strength of the person who will be carrying the bag. You don't want to give your 80-year grandma a pack that weighs 50 pounds. She isn't going to make it far under that heavy of load unless she's a bodybuilder; then by all means load her up. It helps to keep in mind that you can pack all the gear in the world, but it isn't going to do you any good if it gets too heavy and has to be left behind.

For some, picking the right bag is an agonizing decision. There are literally hundreds of bags on the market, maybe even thousands. You can spend countless hours searching and still not come to a conclusion as to what the best bag for you is.

If you're one of those people, here's what I suggest. Go to your local department store right now and buy an inexpensive backpack that fits your torso. Bring it home and pack as much gear as you can into it. Now you've got as much time as you want to research and won't fill pressed to make a quick decision. You've got a bag ready to go if you need it, which is the most important thing. Once you start packing gear into your bag, you're going to notice things you do and don't like about the bag. This will give you a baseline to use when you start shopping for a better bag. You can upgrade the bag later once you've narrowed down your needs.

There are two things you ideally want your bug out bag to be. That's lightweight and durable. In the cheaper bags, those two items are mutually exclusive of one another. You might find cheaper bags that are light or cheaper bags that are durable, but you're going to have to spend big bucks to get the best of both worlds. The more lighter and durable you want your bag to be, the more it's going to cost you.

How to Pick the Right Size Bag

Figure 2: This backpack is NOT the right size.

Camping backpack frames are sized based on the size of your torso, not how tall you are. A person who is 6'1" might assume he needs a large/tall backpack, but that isn't always the case. A person with a smaller torso and long legs may need a smaller bag.

To figure out what size backpack you need, measure the distance from the base of your neck to your hipbone. This is your torso size. In order to get an accurate measurement, you're going to need to enlist the help of a friend. Bend your head forward and have your friend find the spinal bump on the back of your neck near where the neck meets the back. This is your starting point. Now, put your hands on your hips and push in while sliding your hands up until you find the top of your hip bone. This is the point you want to measure to.

When you go to buy a bag, you want to keep this measurement handy. Most manufacturers use the following guidelines to size their bags:

Bag Size	Torso Size
Extra small	Up to 15 ½"
Small	16" to 17 ½"
Regular	18" to 19"
Large/Tall	20" and up

If your measurements are smaller than what's shown above, you can look into getting a children's backpack. If you're torso is bigger than about 22", you're going to have to look for a specialty bag for taller people. I know REI has at least one bag that's made for torsos of up to 23". Any bigger than that and you're going to have to get a frame custom built.

It's a good idea to always check the labels before you buy a bag because there are a few manufacturers who don't adhere to this standard.

The holding capacity of a backpack is measured in liter size. The liter size tells you how approximately how much gear you can jam in the backpack. For a 3-day BOB you want at least a 50L bag. If you have a strong back and need to carry a lot of gear, you can go as high as 80L. Just be aware a bag of this size is going to be extremely heavy if you fill it up.

It's tough to decide which backpack to buy, especially when you consider the fact that a good hiking backpack can cost you hundreds of dollars. Here's a list of some bags you may want to consider:

Osprey Hornet (Approximately $130 to $170)

This super light bag comes in two sizes: 24L and 46L. The larger of the two sizes weighs in at just over a pound. Its ergonomic design eliminates most of the framing found on heavier bags. The capacity is a bit smaller than what you probably want unless you're an ultralight camper who knows how to travel light. This bag is a good option for older children and those who aren't able to handle heavier bags.

Granite Gear Crown V.C. 60 ($199.95)

This lightweight back has a bit more capacity. It carries a capacity of 60L and weighs in at 1 pound, 13 ounces. The frame can be removed from the bag if you want to go ultralight.

Summit 2800 Ultralite ($75.00)

This budget entry from Teton Sports weighs in at 3.2 pounds and carries a 45L capacity. It's a good choice for the budget minded consumer looking for a relatively light bag.

GoLite Quest 80L Pack ($109.99)

Looking to go big on capacity? This pack carries an 80L capacity and weighs in at just 3 pounds, 12 ounces. It has a perimeter frame that the manufacturer says transfers the weight to your hips instead of your back.

Teton Sports Fox5200 Internal Frame ($79.99)

If you're on a budget and want an inexpensive bag with a lot of capacity, you could do a lot worse than the Teton Sports Fox5200. This bag holds 85L and weighs in at just 5.5 pounds.

Maxpedition Vulture II ($169.99)

Now we're moving into the heavy-duty gear. The Maxpedition Vulture II has a 46L capacity and weighs 3 pounds 8 ounces. You can attach additional gear to sewn nylon hard points on the outside of the pack.

Alps Mountaineering Zion External Frame ($159.99)

This external frame bag is built to last and has a capacity of just under 64L. It's a little heavy though, as it weighs in at 4 pounds, 15 ounces.

Denali Pro 105 ($548.00)

If you're looking to go big or go home and don't mind feeling like a pack mule, the Denali Pro 105 might be the answer to your prayers. Depending on your torso size, you can get up to 115L of capacity. You'd better have a strong back if you plan on filling this bag. The bag alone weighs 8 pounds.

Gregory Deva 70 ($319.00)

Looking for a light bag with extra capacity for the women in your group? This bag can carry up to 73L of goods and only weighs 5 pounds, 15 ounces. While it's designed with women in mind, it's a decent choice for anyone looking for a light bag that can carry a lot of gear.

Three Day Pass Bugout Backpack ($50.00)

The manufacturer doesn't appear to have a website, but this bag is available for around $50 at a number of online stores. This military-spec bag carries a smaller capacity (35L) than most hiking backpacks but is designed to look like a normal backpack. You can easily blend into an urban environment while carrying enough gear to survive on for 3 days.

ROTHCO G.I. Type CFP-90 Combat Pack ($160.99)

This pack is a better-than-mil-spec replica of a U.S. military pack. It's heavy-duty and can hold all the survival gear you'll need. It comes in either camouflage or black.

Osprey Argon 110 ($359)

The Osprey Argon 110 carries between 110L and 116L capacity and weighs less than 7 pounds. It's a bit pricey, but is a good choice if you want durability, capacity and a light weight bag all in one. The Argon series also comes in 85L and 70L capacities for those who don't want to bring everything but the kitchen sink along when they bug out.

Granite Gear CHIEF Recce ($699)

This is the cream of the crop when it comes to bug out bags. It meets U.S. Special Ops Forces requirements and is capable of carrying 110L. Before you run out and buy it, consider whether you're in good enough shape to carry one of these bags. The bag alone weighs in at 7 pounds, 9 ounces. It can weigh as much as a hundred pounds when fully loaded.

Where to Store Your Bug Out Bag

Figure 3: Don't bury your bag in the back of a closet.

Ideally, you'd keep your bug out bag right next to your front door or garage door so you could grab it on your way out the door in the event of an emergency. This would allow you to evacuate your home in the shortest amount of time possible.

You'd have a bag for each family member who could carry one all lined up neatly down the hall. The family would line up and each person would grab their bag on the way out the door, and then toss it in the trunk of the vehicle you're going to escape in.

The reality is most people aren't going to want to store backpacks in the hallway. Or you might want to, but your significant other won't let you. Or you're too scared to even ask. Regardless of the reason, the hallway probably isn't going to happen unless you want to end up single.

A hall closet might be a good compromise that'll keep you out of divorce court. You'll still be storing your gear close to the exit, but now it's out of sight. It'll take a few seconds extra to open the door, but at least you don't have to worry about running around the house grabbing the stuff you need. It'll all be in a single location right by the exit.

If you keep your vehicles in the garage, store your gear right there in the garage. Hang your bags from the wall so they'll be easy to get to and you won't have to move a pile of junk every time you want to check your inventory.

Avoid placing your bags in areas that are tough to get to. You don't want to have to take multiple trips up to the far corner of the attic when you're in a hurry to get out of your house. You also don't want to take multiple trips to a detached garage or a shed in your backyard. Find a place close to the exit you'll be using and you'll save precious seconds during an evacuation.

Wherever you decide to store your bag, it needs to be accessible. Make a steadfast rule that nothing gets placed on or around your gear and stick to it. A bug out bag that you can't get to in the event of an emergency is just as bad as not having a bag at all.

How Heavy Can Your Bag Be?

You don't want to be weighted down by a bag that has you right on the verge of toppling over. Your back isn't going to last one day, let alone three. Even the healthiest of people will hurt themselves trying to carry too heavy of a load.

The size bag you can carry can be figured out as a percentage of your body weight calculated based on what kind of physical shape you're in.

A person in poor health may not realistically be able to lift anything. To be bluntly honest with you, the hike to a bug location alone may be a death sentence for those in poor health. You need to realistically assess what the people in your group can handle and plan accordingly. Taking grandma who has a heart problem and emphysema up a steep mountain trail probably isn't going to end with everyone reaching the destination alive and safe.

Those in moderate health can carry from 10% to 15% of their body weight. A person weighing 200 pounds who is out of shape may be able to handle a 30-pound bag. A person who's in good health and is physically fit can handle 25%, which equates to a 50-pound bag for a 200-pound person. An experienced backpacker can hit the trail wearing as much as 35% of their body weight. That's a 70-pound bag for a 200-pound person.

Be realistic when assessing how heavy of a bag you can carry. Take health factors like asthma, diabetes and leg and back problems into consideration. Smokers are going to have to pack lighter, as are heavy drinkers and drug users.

Even if you're in the prime of your life and are in peak physical condition, you probably aren't going to want to lug a 70-pound bag around. It's going to make for a miserable existence. Pack as light as you can pack without leaving critically-important items behind.

Most people overestimate how heavy of a bag they can handle. They buy the biggest bag they can find and fill it up. Then they try it on, walk around the house with it on for a couple minutes and assume it's OK. This method of testing a bag's weight fails on multiple levels. You need to take your bag to your bug out location and carry it around for *a couple hours* to get a good idea of whether or not you can handle it. A quick pass through the house on level terrain doesn't cut it.

Water: Staying Hydrated Is the Key to Staying Alive

Figure 4: Scout out water sources in the area you're bugging out to ahead of time.

The human body relies on water like it relies on no other substance. Your body uses water for the following functions:

- **Thins the blood.** Your blood is made up of 90% water.
- **Brain function.** Your brain is 85% water.
- **Helps dissolve nutrients into a form the body can use.**
- **Digestion.**
- **Flushes out waste products.**

- **Lubricates joints.**
- **Protects organs and tissue.**
- **Keeps mouth, eyes and nose moist.**
- **Sweat cools the body down when it starts to heat up.**
- **Regulates body temperature.**

The human body can't survive without a constant supply of water. Dehydration can set in within an hour if you're exerting yourself on a hot day. If you're sweating profusely and aren't replacing the water you're losing, you can die within hours of becoming dehydrated.

Not drinking enough water can result in the following problems:

- **Dry mouth.**
- **Dry eyes.**
- **Dry skin.**
- **Eyes sink into sockets.**
- **Heartbeat speeds up.**
- **Body slows down.**
- **Lack of perspiration.**
- **Diarrhea.**
- **Digestive problems.**
- **Constipation.**
- **Vomiting.**
- **Headache.**
- **Stomachache.**
- **Brain damage.**
- **Bloating.**

- **Fever.**
- **Stressed internal organs because there isn't enough water to flush out toxins.**
- **Blood pressure increases.**
- **Organ failure.**
- **Inadequate oxygen supply to muscles and the brain.**
- **Irritability.**
- **Lethargy.**
- **Lack of energy.**
- **Shock.**
- **Death.**

Assuming you're in tip-top shape and aren't overexerting yourself, you might be able to survive 5 days without water. If it's hot and you're trying to get to a distant location, you might not make it through one day without water. You're really going to be pushing your luck after 2. Your body is going to start going into shock, your internal organs will start failing and everything will start shutting down.

Water should be your number one concern when it comes to packing a bug out bag. The bare minimum amount of water you should have is a half-gallon of water per person per day. If you're expecting to be hiking in warm temperatures, you're going to need even more.

The problem with water is it's heavy. A gallon of water weighs just over 8 pounds. The bare minimum amount of water you're going to need per person is a gallon and a half. That means you're going to be carrying at least 20 pounds worth of water alone—and that's for one person. If you have people coming along who can't carry their own bags, your bag is going to increase by 20 pounds of weight for each person you're carrying for.

Water Carrying Systems

Figure 5: Canteens haven't changed much since the 1800's. They're still big, bulky and heavy.

You're going to need to carry water. The amount you need to carry largely depends on where you're headed and how hot it's going to be, but there are few scenarios that don't require you to carry at least some water.

There are a number of water carrying systems on the market today.

You could go old school and fill up a canteen. A canteen is a metal or plastic container that you keep your water in. They'll work in a pinch, but aren't able to carry enough water to be of value. They're bulky and you don't want to have to carry multiple canteens with you. I do carry one that can be filled with water, but I carry it as a means of water purification. More on that in a bit.

Another option is to store bottles of water in your bug out bag. Bottled water lasts a lot longer than the date on the label says it does. You may have noticed the bottles have a shelf life on them, but that's just to keep the state of New Jersey happy. They require water bottles sold there to be labeled with an expiration date even though water doesn't really expire as long as the bottle stays sealed.

Water that's been stored for a long time can take on a plastic taste. This occurs because the chemicals in the plastic start leaching into the water. Another problem with bottled water is the bottles are big and never seem to fit properly into a backpack.

Hydration bladders are probably the number one water storage system used by survivalists. A hydration bladder is a rubber or plastic bladder into which you put water. They commonly hold between 1.5 and 4 liters. It has a locking cap that you remove to fill the bladder. Water bladders are a good choice for a bug out bag because most of them come with a hose attached through which you can drink. You can snake the hose out of your bag and hydrate yourself without having to open your bag and get into it. This will save you precious minutes when you don't have time to stop and get water out of your bag.

If you don't have room in your bag for a water bladder, a *hydration pack* may be a good option. Hydration packs are separate packs that just hold water. There are hydration packs that are made to attach to a backpack; just make sure you remember to factor the weight of the fully loaded hydration pack into your bag weight. A full hydration pack can weigh as much as 30 pounds.

There are 2 general schools of thought when it comes to storing water bladders or hydration packs in bug out bags. The first line of thinking states you should store your bags empty and fill them up with fresh water when you bug out. This ensures you get fresh water straight from the tap and not water that's sat around so long it's gone tepid.

This isn't a good idea because you may find yourself in a situation in which you don't have time to fill up a bunch of bags. You'll either have to put yourself in danger by staying put long enough to fill your bags or you'll have to leave without filling them. There aren't many bug out worthy situations in which time isn't of essence. You aren't going to want to waste precious minutes filling your bags.

There's also the possibility that you may be evacuating because of an emergency that's contaminated the water supply. It may sound far-fetched, but disaster preparedness requires you to look at all possible angles and be ready for whatever may be thrown your way. Just off the top of my head, I can name multiple scenarios in which your water supply may be contaminated. There could be a toxic waste spill. A truck or train could derail and dump chemicals into the water supply. A terrorist could poison or irradiate the water supply. There are a lot of potential crisis situations you're ignoring if you're storing your bags empty and planning on filling them up when you leave.

The second school of thought when it comes to filling hydration bladders is that you should fill your bags and store them full. This isn't a great idea either. Your water is going to need to be changed constantly, and if you're anything like me, you're going to forget to change it. By the time you remember, it's going to be a nasty, slimy mess of algae and bacteria. If you don't remember and bug out with water that's gone bad, you could end up in the middle of nowhere without a ready supply of water.

You could also end up drinking a chemical cocktail of contaminants that have leached out of the plastic or rubber into your water. The longer your water is stored, the higher the risk of chemicals leaching into the water. Would it stop me from drinking it if I had to bug out and had no other option? No, but I'd prefer not to if I don't have to.

So, we've storing water bladders full and storing them empty and neither is a perfect choice. You either run the risk of not having time to fill your bags or you have to constantly monitor your water supply to make sure it isn't going bad.

There's another option that will make life much easier on you while ensuring you have the water you need.

Buy a water bladder and fill it up. Let it sit for a day or two and wash it out. Repeat the process. This will rinse at least some of the chemical residue from the inside of the bag. It's going to be a pain in the butt, but you need to make absolutely sure you dry all of the water out of the bag. Once it's dry, store it on top of your bug out bag.

Instead of storing your water inside the hydration bladder where it can go bad, get a couple sealed jugs of water and store them next to your bug out bags. When you grab your bags to bug out, grab the bottles and the bladders sitting on top of your bags and throw them in the cab of the car. You can fill the bladders up while you're driving to your destination. Chances are, there's going to be traffic headed the same way you are and you'll have plenty of time to fill the bags on the way out of town.

This method will slow you down a bit because you have extra stuff to grab, but it won't slow you down as much as taking the time to fill your bladders before you leave. Rotate your plastic bottles every six months or so and you won't have to worry about your water picking up chemicals from the plastic. You'll have all the water you need stored by the bags and you eliminate most of the negative issues associated with storing it there.

Water Purification Can Help You Lighten Your Load and May Save Your Life

Figure 6: Would you be willing to drink this water? With a water purification device, you could if you had to.

Most bug out bags contain enough water to last for three days, give or take a day or two, but what happens if you end up having to rely on nothing but the supplies in your bag for a week or even a month. Could you do it? Probably not without a water purification device.

There's no good reason not to carry a water purification device in your bug out bag. They're relatively inexpensive, they're lightweight and they exponentially expand the places you can procure water from in the wilderness.

I often hear people say they've scouted the area they plan on bugging out to and there's plenty of running water in the area. There's a common misconception going around that running water equates to clean water. Whenever I hear someone say this, I start pulling up images on my phone of rivers where there's running water, but no one in their right mind would drink from them without first treating the water.

Tell me, would you want to drink from any of these rivers?

I don't know about you, but I wouldn't want to drink from any of them without purifying the water first. Even then, it might be a little sketchy.

I know what you're thinking right now.

The running water you've scouted looks a heck of a lot cleaner than the water in the pictures above. Clean-looking running water is a safer bet than tepid standing water, but you never know what lurks beneath the surface. Even perfectly clear water in a bubbling brook a hundred miles from civilization can be rife with harmful microorganisms.

Planning on heading for the mountains and using snow as a water source? Think again. Snow can get contaminated by airborne particles or animals tracking feces through it. It's a good idea to purify snow before you melt it and drink it.

All water that doesn't come from a known clean source should be treated before you drink it. All of it. If you've been out to your bug out location and have scouted water sources and tried the water to see if it was OK, consider yourself very lucky that you didn't get sick. E. coli, giardia, worms, dysentery and parasites are only a few of the microorganisms and bacteria known to reside in untreated water.

Even if you're 100% sure your water supply is good, you should treat it. Here's why.

Picture yourself arriving at a small clearing next to a babbling brook you've been following for a few miles and deciding this is a good place to call it a night. You've been here before and you've sampled the water a few different times to make sure it was clean. You didn't get sick any of the other times, so you assume the water is still going to be good.

Your assumptions are dead wrong.

Unbeknownst to you, 200 yards upstream lies a moose carcass blocking the little stream. It's so big it dams almost the entire stream. The water pools up behind it and trickles around it on both sides. It's been there for a while and is badly decomposed. Every once in a while a small chunk of the rotting carcass breaks off and tumbles down the stream.

You find the carcass the next morning, right after waking up and drinking copiously of the refreshing water. An hour later your stomach starts turning and you begin to feel sick. You've just placed yourself in a very dangerous situation— and it's one you could have avoided with a little common sense.

To make water safe, you need to do two things to it:

- **Filter it to get rid of large particles.**
- **Treat it to get rid of microorganisms.**

To complete these two tasks, you only need a few items, some of which you should already have in your bug out bag. The items you need are:

- **A filter.** You can carry a small filter in your BOB. Coffee filters will work. So will a bandana or piece of cloth. You can even use a tampon.
- **A source of water.** If you've done your homework, you'll know of a few places along your route where you can find water. Google Maps is a good place to start. Once you've located likely sources on the map, get out there and check them out. All isn't always as it seems in the pictures. Streams, ponds and even lakes can all dry up during a drought. Make sure you scout your water sources when they're most likely to be dry. You can find all kinds of water in the winter. Finding water at the end of a long, hot summer might be a different story.
- **A canteen.** You can store water in your canteen. As long as you have a metal canteen, it serves double

duty as a pot in which you can boil your water, which is one way you can sterilize it.

- **Fire.** You need to be able to start a fire in the wilderness, both with and without matches or a lighter. Fire can be used to boil water and is the most basic way you can sterilize water for consumption.

Once you find a source of water, place your filter over the mouth of the canteen and pour the water slowly through the filter to fill the canteen up. Get your fire going real good and place your canteen in or over the fire. Make sure you remove the canteen's cloth or rubber cover before heating it up. Bring the water inside the canteen to a boil and let it boil for a couple minutes. Once you've had the water boiling for 1 minute it should be safe, but boiling it for an extra minute or two for good measure isn't going to hurt.

Bringing water to a boil to sterilize it is one of the oldest and most effective methods, but it isn't the only game in town. Here's a list of options you can choose for water sterilization:

- **Filters.** There are a number of filters on the market you can use to make your water safe. The cheaper filters have bigger pores and will still let viruses sneak through. The more expensive filters have pores that are as small as .01 microns. The smaller the pores, the less likely the filter is to let contaminants and viruses through. You may want to use a filter to remove the larger particles and finish sterilizing your water with one of the other methods listed.

- **Chemicals.** Chemical treatments can be used to kill microorganisms. 3 drops of liquid chlorine bleach in a quart of water will kill everything in it within 10 minutes. Make sure the bleach you use isn't stronger than 5 or 6 percent chlorine and shake it up real good. Be careful not to use too much because it can make you very sick. Avoid bleaches with perfumes, scents or dyes. There are also water purification pills you can buy and keep in your bug out bag. The problem with chemical treatments is they're only good for one use. Once the chemicals have been used up, you're not going to be able to purify your water.

- **Ultraviolet (UV) treatments.** UV light can be used to kill off microorganisms. You can clean clear water by placing it in a clear PET container and leaving it out in bright sunlight for 6 to 8 hours. Plastic other than PET may inhibit the ability of UV rays to penetrate through the plastic. You can speed up the process with a traveler's water purifying pen or stick. These devices use UV-C light rays to sterilize water in matter of minutes. They work well and a single purifier can be used up to a couple thousand times before it needs to be replaced. The problem is they burn through batteries at a fast clip. Batteries are heavy and add a lot of weight to your bag.

If you have a method of water purification and a ready supply of water, you can lighten your load a bit as long as you're confident the water will be there when you need it. I don't recommend carrying much less than 1 ½ gallons per person, but when it comes to your bug out bag, every ounce counts.

Don't make the mistake of assuming you're going to be able to rely on boiling your water. In order to use this method, you have to have time to build a fire and you have to be in a location where it's safe to build one. If you're running from someone or something, you're going to lose valuable time if you have to stop and build a fire every time you need water. The smoke could give away your location and trackers will be watching for the flicker of a fire at night.

Keep a small, lightweight filtration system in your bag with a few extra batteries. Don't use it unless you have to and you'll be able to make a quick escape if the time comes where you have to go on the run.

Desalination: You Can Drink Salt Water

Picture this. You're on an island surrounded by water and you're dying of thirst. Your lips and mouth are dry and cracked and your throat is burning with every breath you take. You've heard the stories about drinking salt water, but it's so tempting and looks so refreshing.

If you're planning on bugging out to an area where there's salt water like an island or somewhere close to ocean, you're going to want to have a way to desalinate salt water.

Sea-Pack sells a hand-held desalinator that'll fit in a backpack. It'll process half a liter of water within 4 hours and even adds a bit of sugar to it, which speeds up the process and provides you with a quick energy boost. If you have the room for it, the Sea-Pack is a great tool to have on hand.

If money isn't an option, you can go with a handheld pump unit like the Katadyn Survivor 06 Desalinator. This hand-operated pump can be used to desalinate up to a gallon of drinkable water in less than an hour. It's going to weigh you down a bit. It clocks in at 7 pounds, which is light for a desalinator, but not light for a BOB. One thing it won't weigh down in your wallet. The Katadyn Survivor 06 will set you back nearly $900.

Another option is a solar still. You could learn to make your own or you can pack a ready-to-go one in your bag. Aquamate makes one that weighs just over 2 pounds. It's still a little pricy at nearly $240, but it's a fraction of the cost of the Katadyn unit.

Food

I talked to a guy recently who told me he doesn't keep food in his bug out bag. He said he has enough water to last for three days and that's all he needs. This guy is the John Rambo-type, who would go out and tough it out for 3 days without food just so he could say he did it.

The human body can survive for weeks without food, so his premise was there's no reason to pack food in a bag intended to help you survive just three days.

While he's technically correct, you're going to be pretty miserable after the first 24 hours without food. Your stomach will feel like it's being twisted in knots and all you'll be able to think about is how hungry you are. You won't be able to think straight and will be more likely to make a mistake that could cost you your life.

Don't believe me? Try to go one day without eating any food at all. How did you feel by the end of the day? Now, imagine hiking all day in the hot sun with no food. You'd probably live through the day if you're healthy and you have water, but it's a miserable existence.

You're not going to need a lot of food for three days, but you're going to want to have at least some.

Ready-to-eat meals (MREs) are one option. They're basically meals that you can open and eat without having to prepare or cook them in any way. You can grab one and chow it down and be back on the trail in minutes. The best part about MREs is they taste good, as long as you like the taste of flavored Styrofoam.

Some MREs come with a small flameless ration heater, so you'll be able to warm your food up before you eat it without having to build a fire. These heaters are good for one use only, but are small enough that you can pack a few.

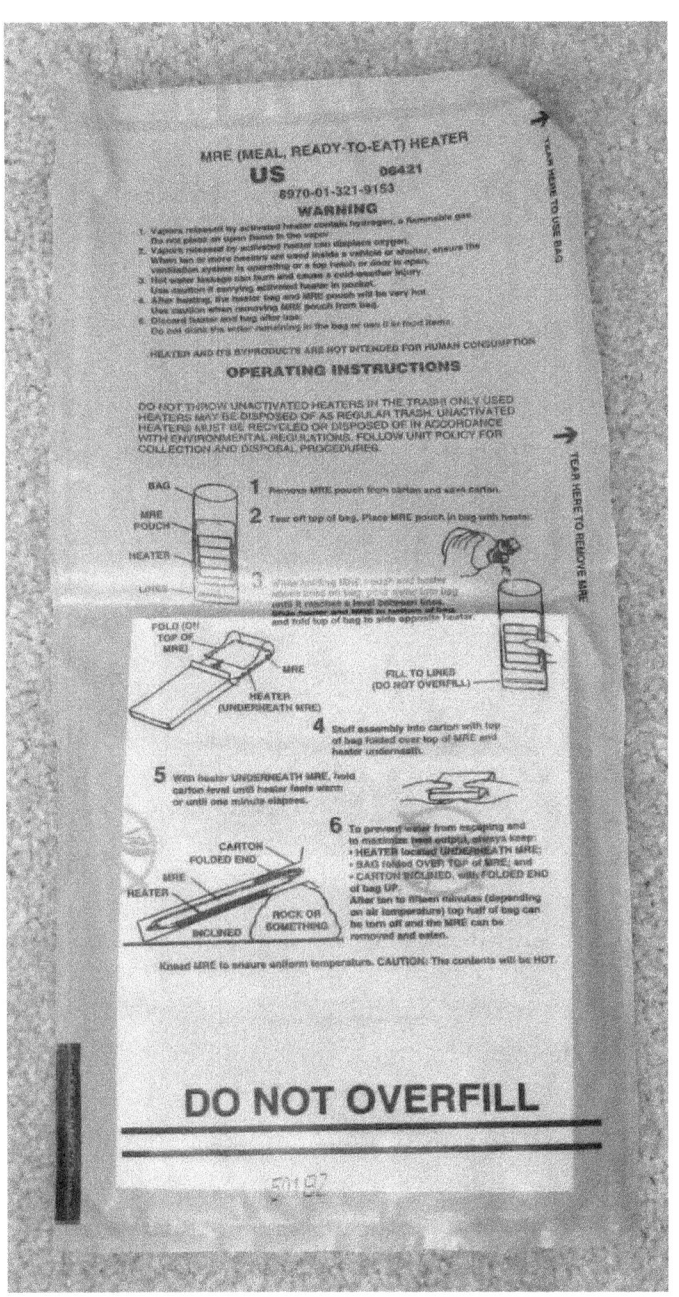

Figure 7: MRE heater.

If your MREs didn't come with a heater, you can throw a few hand-warmers in your bag. They'll work every bit as well.

MREs aren't cheap. They'll run you around $6 bucks a meal. If you have a family of 6, that's 18 meals you have to buy, which equates to 108 bucks for meals for a family of 6. Doesn't sound too bad, right? It wouldn't be if they lasted longer than 3 years. The average MRE needs to be replaced every 3 years if stored in a cool, dry place. If they're stored in a warm place or a place with high humidity, you might find yourself having to replace them every 6 months. If you're keeping your bug out bags in your garage or in a shed, you're going to be replacing your MREs more often than you'd like.

Another problem with MREs is their weight. They're heavy and bulky. The upside is just one can sustain you for an entire day, but it isn't going to fill you up. MREs are full of sodium and low in fiber, so they aren't a good long-term food solution. A couple days' worth of MREs are all you're going to want to eat unless you want to end up badly constipated and uncomfortable.

Freeze-dried foods are probably the best option for a bug out bag. They're lightweight and will last forever and a day because almost all of the moisture content has been removed from the food. They don't taste great, but all you need to do is add water back to them and you've got a passable meal that will stave off hunger and provide you a bit of nutrition.

Another good option for keeping hunger at bay is energy bars. The protein bars sold at health food and sporting goods stores are dense bars packed full of nutrients. You can nibble on a bar throughout the day without having to stop and eat a meal if you're pressed for time.

I'd suggest packing enough freeze dried food to last you three days, along with a few protein bars to eat on the go. Forget about the MREs unless you have a personal preference for them.

Figure 8: Even if you don't have hunting and fishing gear with you, you can build a deadfall trap from branches and trees.

I know bug out bags are supposed to contain enough gear to get you through 3 days in the wild. If you bring enough food, you'll be able to get through 3 days without needing to hunt or fish. But what happens if you end up having to stay longer than three days? Could you survive a week, a month or even a year in the wild?

With the right supplies and little luck, you probably could.

If there are lakes, rivers or even small streams nearby, you're going to want a way to harvest the fish in them. You could build traps or try to spear fish swimming close to shore, but catching them with fishing line is a heck of a lot easier.

I recommend keeping two types of fishing line in your bug out bag. Keep a light 6- to 8-pound test monofilament and a heavy 60- to 80-pound braid. You're going to want 30 to 40 feet of each. The smaller diameter monofilament can be used in clear-water lakes and streams where fish may be line-shy. They may take bait off of a light line where they'd ignore it on a heavier line. Fluorocarbon line is almost invisible when it's in the water and is worth the extra buck or two it'll cost you.

The heavy braided line can be used to set up a trot line, which is a single line with multiple hooks attached to it that'll really up your chances of catching something. You might be able to catch 4 or 5 fish at once with a trot line. Try attaching the end of the trot line to something that floats and using the wind to float it out away from shore.

Trot lines can also be used to catch other animals like turtles and ducks. Try floating a trot line with Cheetos hooked to it in an area where ducks are present and you might catch yourself a nice dinner. I keep a small bag of Cheetos in my BOB just in case. It doesn't add any weight at all and I can eat them if there aren't any ducks around. Ducks will also eat worms, insects, small fish and all sorts of other stuff, so if you don't have Cheetos, don't worry about it. String a few worms on the trot line, float it away from shore and hope for the best.

You're going to need fishing hooks, so throw a few packs of them in your bag. You might want to throw a bobber or two in there as well so you can see when you get a bite. I've also got a few flies that I know catch fish in the mountains I plan on bugging out to. I hook these through the brim of my hat to save space.

If you aren't sure which flies work in your area, stop by your local tackle shop with one of your kids in tow. They'll be more likely to give up the good information if you have a kid along.

Some people like to pack a telescoping fishing rod in their bag. I've found the telescoping rods aren't worth their weight in graphite and I get more mileage from whittling down a sapling and using it. I'm not out there trying to land Moby Dick. I'm perfectly happy with a bunch of pan-size fish. If I do hook a big one, I'm going in after it!

As far as hunting goes, you have a few options.

You should have some sort of rifle or shotgun for protection. This can serve double purpose as a hunting tool as long as you aren't worried about someone hearing the shots. You won't be able to pack a lot of ammo because of its weight, so you're going to be limited as to how much food you can shoot. The more ammo you use to hunt game, the less you're going to have to defend yourself with.

You can pack a few feet of thin rabbit wire and set up a snare along paths where game animals travel. A simple snare loop looks like this:

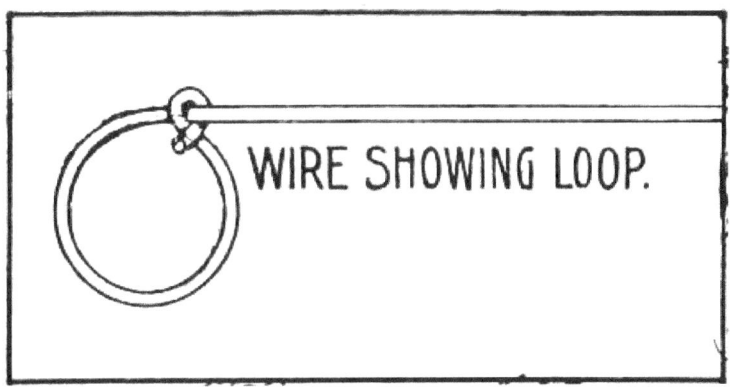

You can open up the loop and set it in a well-worn game path and hope an unlucky animal comes wandering by and gets his neck caught in it.

There are a number of snares and traps you can make using twine, wire, rocks and/or sticks. If you'd like to learn more about trapping game, I recommend reading "Deadfalls and Snares" by A.R. Harding. It's an old book, but the information is still good. Just be careful not to practice setting any of the traps in areas where other people, children or pets could wander into them. Some of them are capable of killing or maiming large mammals—that includes us.

Here's a link to a free online version of the book:

http://www.gutenberg.org/files/34110/34110-h/34110-h.htm

The traps in the book require that you either bait them or set them up in an area animals routinely pass through. It can take a fair bit of time to trap an animal, especially in the winter months, so make sure you give yourself plenty of time.

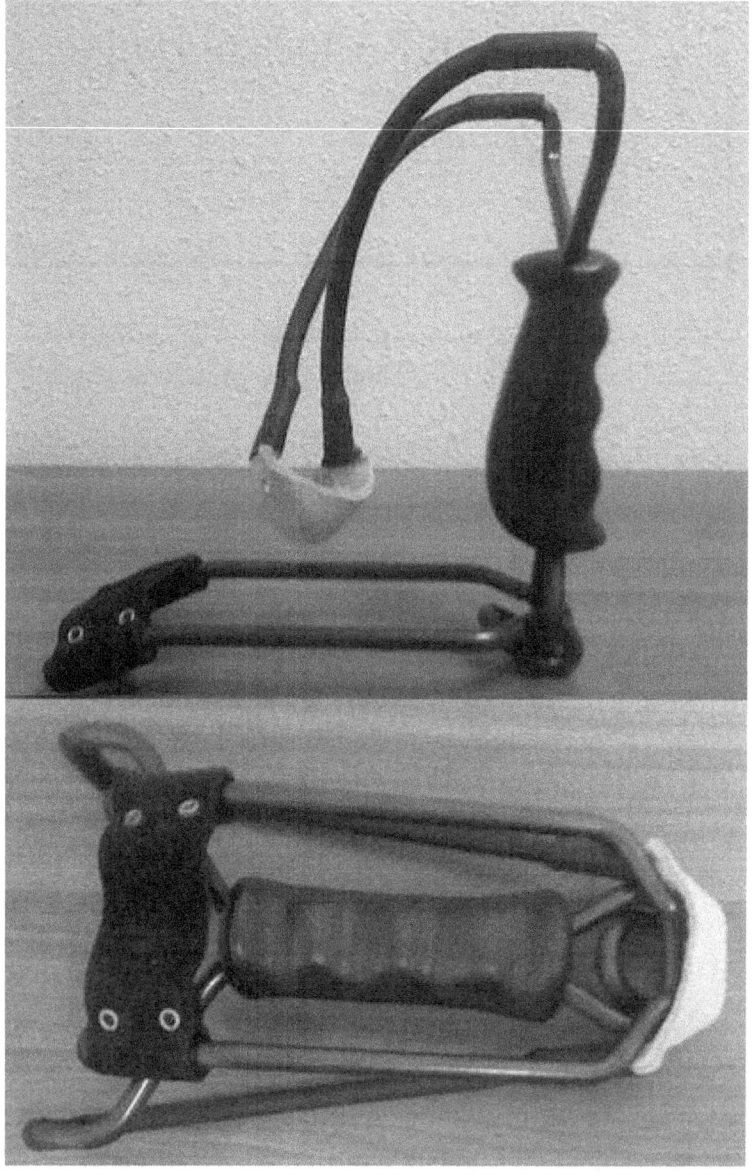

Figure 9: A folding slingshot is a good item to use to hunt small game.

There's always the concern you'll have to stay mobile and won't have time to bait traps and wait for an animal to find them. You can carry a lightweight folding slingshot with you that will allow you to kill small game fairly easily. The ball ammo for the slingshot can really weigh your bag down, so instead of carrying ball ammo, you can collect a handful of smaller rocks when it's time to go hunting. They track almost as well as the ball ammo at the distances at which you'll be hunting.

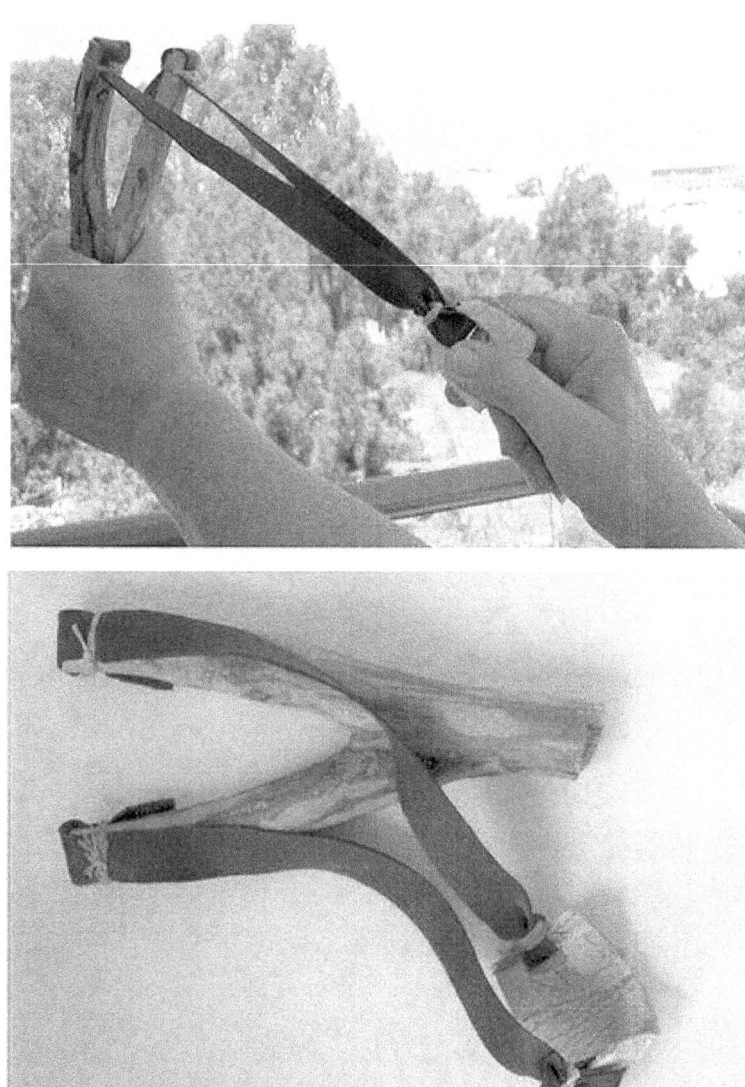

Figure 10: Primitive homemade slingshot.

You can make your own slingshot if you're feeling industrious. All you need is flexible rubber tubing or a thick rubber band, a forked stick, some twine and a piece of leather for the pocket. Take a look at the slingshot in the image above. It's simplistic, but will make for an effective weapon capable of killing animals as large as raccoons.

Protection from the Elements

Unless you live in a place where the climate is mild year-round, you're going to want some sort of shelter you can hunker down in to wait out inclement weather. In most bug out areas, the weather can get nasty in a hurry. I've been in the mountains in the middle of July and been caught in a full on lightning storm with torrential downpours.

Shelter also provides a barrier between you and roving wildlife at night. Snakes, scorpions, spiders, raccoons and predatory animals of all types have no problem wandering through a campsite at night. The smaller creatures have no problems sneaking into a nice, warm sleeping bag to cozy up against a warm body. They also have no problem biting or stinging when that warm body realizes it isn't alone and starts squirming and trying to get out of the bag.

Some people are willing to get by with just a tarp. I'm not. The area I live in is crawling with insects, tarantulas and snakes and a tent provides me an extra barrier between me and them.

The best tents for backpacking are the ultra-light tents. There are a number of great tents out there. Single-wall tents are the lightest, but they don't provide much of a barrier between you and the elements. Double-wall tents are a bit heavier, but have a second barrier designed to prevent moisture from condensing on the inside of the tent.

Solo tents are going to be lighter than tents designed for multiple people. If you have multiple people traveling in your group, you may be better off carrying 2-man tents that are slightly heavier. A single 2-man tent will be lighter than two 1-man tents and you'll be able to huddle together to stay warm on cold nights. That is, if you're going with someone you want to huddle up with. I'd rather freeze than share a tent with some of my friends.

Most ultra-light tents come with lightweight aluminum poles. You may be able to shave a few ounces off of each pole by switching over to carbon fiber poles.

The lightest tents I've seen are ZPack's Hexamid Tents. The Hexamid Twin sleeps two people and weighs in at just over a pound—and that includes the tent, bag, 2 carbon fiber poles (which have to bought separately) and a lightweight ground cover (also sold separately). A tent this light doesn't come cheap. It costs $415.00 for the tent alone. Add in the stakes and ground cover and you'll be over $500 easy.

For a couple hundred bucks, you can get lightweight tents from places like Mountain Hardware, REI or North Face. The mid-range priced ultra-lights will run from 3 ½ to 4 ½ pounds.

In addition to a tent, you're going to need a tarp or some sort of ground cover to place between the tent and the ground. This will prevent moisture from evaporating from the ground into your tent and causing condensation on the inside. This is a critical component and can't be forgotten. You don't want to wake up to find everything inside your tent sopping wet.

The Sleeping Bag

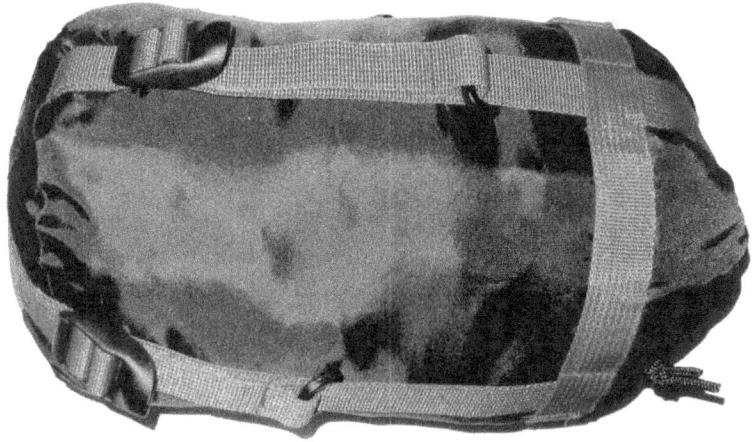

Figure 11: A compression sack will get your bag down to about 4" in diameter and 9 inches long.

A lightweight sleeping bag stuffed into a compression sack is able to be attached to the outside of your bug out bag and doesn't add a whole lot of weight or bulk to your bag. Couple a compression sack with a lightweight bag and you probably won't even feel the extra weight.

In order to pick the right bag for you, you're going to have to know what the nightly low temperatures are that you're likely to see in the area where you plan on staying.

I don't recommend using the average nightly low temperatures when deciding what bag to buy. The average low temperature would be fine if every night stayed at that temperature. It doesn't. Some nights are warmer and some might be significantly colder than the average low temperature on record. If you go with the average low temperature and find yourself camping out on the coldest night of the year, you're going to be sorry you didn't spring for a warmer bag.

I'd look at the coldest temperatures on record and get a bag that can handle them. You can thank me when you're out in the wild in the middle of January and are nice and cozy in your 0 degree bag.

You can find bags that are good down to 20 degrees that weigh less than a pound. If you need a bag that's good down to zero degrees, there are a number of them that weigh less than 1 ½ pounds. You can get a good sub-zero bag that clocks in at 2 to 3 pounds.

I don't recommend going too cheap on your sleeping bag unless you want to spend miserable nights shivering in the cold. Down filling is probably going to be your best bet when it comes to packing a light sleeping bag that's going to keep you warm. It's more expensive than all but the best synthetic fillings and it compresses well and can be stuffed into a small bag.

Speaking of compression bags, there's a lot of debate as to whether it's best to store a sleeping bag compressed in a compression sack or whether it's best to leave it uncompressed until it's time to go. The concern with storing a bag compressed is that the filling may compress permanently over time and degrade to the point where the bag will no longer keep you as warm as what it's rated for.

I've tried it both ways and prefer to keep my bags stored compressed and attached to my BOB. It takes time to stuff a sleeping bag into a compression sack and leaving it sitting out uncompressed just adds one more thing I have to remember if there's an emergency.

If you're really worried about the compression ruining your bag, keep multiple bags and always have at least one of them ready at a moment's notice. You can keep a winter bag and a summer bag and rotate them in and out each season. A bag that's starting to lose its fluff can often be brought back to life by running it through the washing machine. Oils from the human body build up in the bag over time and washing them away can return a bag to its former glory.

Another option is to stuff them into the sack, but don't compress it. You can tighten it up when it's time to bug out. Or you can just use a *stuff sack*. This is a sack into which you stuff your sleeping bag, but it doesn't get compressed. Stuff sacks are bigger and bulkier, but they don't add any weight. If you have room for one, it might be a good compromise.

Down handles being compressed better than synthetic material does. It can be compressed smaller with less chance of fluff degradation at the smaller sizes. I wouldn't recommend using a hydraulic winch to compress your down bag, but a little compression probably isn't going to hurt anything.

I've heard storied of people stuffing their sleeping bags into the bottom of their BOBS and compressing them as they add items to the bug out bag. I don't think this is a good idea because there's too much of a chance of puncturing the bag or tearing a hole in it.

Clothing: Don't Leave With Nothing but the Clothes on Your Back

Figure 12: A good waterproof jacket can be the difference between staying warm and dry and being soaked and miserable in a storm.

It's tempting to say to hell with it, I'm only going to be out there a few days; I can survive in just the clothes I'm wearing for that long. After all, we wore the same clothes for that long while in college and it didn't bother us a bit. Right, guys? Guys? OK, maybe I was the only one.

You're going to want at least one change of warm clothes, maybe two. Any more than that and you're wasting space. Any less and you're putting yourself at risk.

You'll be a lot more comfortable being able to change into clean clothes and the situation may arrive where you end up needing them. If you have to ford a river or you're caught in a downpour that soaks you, you're going to be thankful you packed a change of clothes. You'll be able to change into your clean, dry clothes while you dry your wet clothes out by the fire. You'll also be glad you packed a change of clothes if your shirt gets caught on a sharp branch and gets torn wide open or your pants split at the seams.

Here is the bare minimum that you want to pack in addition to the clothes you're wearing:

- **Long johns.** It can get cold on the trail and a pair of thermal underwear can be a lifesaver. Polypropylene thermal wear is a good choice for staying warm, with the added bonus that it keeps you insulated even when doused with water.
- **2 pairs of clean undies.**
- **A hat.** The type of hat is up to you, but you want something that's going to provide protection from the sun. You don't have to keep this in your bug out

bag. You can just throw it on your head on your way out the door.

- **4 pairs of wool socks.** Avoid cotton socks. Wool socks are much warmer and keep you insulated even when wet. Wool socks retain up to 80% of their insulation even when soaked with water. You want 4 pairs because you can double up when your feet start getting cold. You can also double up your socks to keep from getting blisters.

- **A warm jacket that's waterproof.** The type of jacket you pack should be based on the weather you may encounter. If you can reasonably expect snow and freezing temperatures, you're going to have to pack a warmer jacket than someone bugging out to a tropical climate.

- **Waterproof hiking boots.** Don't pack these in your bag. Keep them next to your bag, so you can put them on when you bug out. Don't use a brand new pair of boots, but don't use an old pair that's on the verge of falling apart either. Buy a pair, wear them until they're broken in and put them with your bug out bag. Don't forget to try them on every six months or so. Even as adults, our foot size can change. You don't want to throw on your boots on your way out the door only to find they're 2 sizes too small.

- **Rain gear.** You can go with something simple like a poncho or go all out and get top of the line Gore-Tex gear. You can cut down on the gear you have to carry by buying a warm jacket that's waterproof. Then all you'll have to do is carry the jacket and a pair of waterproof pants. You can never be too dry in a rain storm. The Frogg Togg line of rain gear is a relatively inexpensive set of gear that'll get the job done. It's comfortable and will keep the rain and wind out, which is all you really need rain gear to do. It's relatively lightweight as far as raingear goes and, best of all, you can get a complete pants and jacket set for less than $50. It isn't real warm though, so it isn't a good choice for colder climates.

- **At least one shirt and one pair of pants.** You need at least one change of outerwear; two if you have room for it.
- **Gloves.** If it's going to be cold, a nice, warm pair of gloves could be the difference between losing fingers to frostbite and arriving at your destination with all of your digits intact. Get a good pair of waterproof gloves to keep your fingers nice and toasty.
- **Bandanas.** This is the Swiss Army knife of your clothing collection. Roll 2 or 3 of them up and stuff them in your bag. They can be used as a tourniquet, to keep the sun off your neck, as a sling, to tie stuff together, as a washcloth or sweatband, to clean firearms, to collect and store stuff, as a dust mask, an eye patch and even as ear muffs, amongst other things. You're going to want a few bandanas on hand. They're light and easy to roll up and won't take up much space. Throw 2 or 3 of them in your bag so you'll have them when and if you need them.
- **Balaclava.** A balaclava can be worn as a hood, a protective head covering, a ski mask and everything

in between. It will help keep your face, head and neck warm in extreme conditions and will protect you from the elements.

When packing clothes into your bug out bag, rolling them up is the best way to make use of the space in the bag without leaving a lot of wasted airspace. Clothes should be rolled up and packed into the bottom of the bag. The rolled up articles of clothing will fit snugly against one another in the bottom of the bag. If you try to jam them in later after putting other stuff in the bag, you're going to have a lot of wasted space.

First Aid

There are so many possibly scenarios in which you might need to administer first aid to a party member that it's impossible to prepare for everything. What you pack in your first aid kit is going to largely depend on where you're bugging out to and the skill level of the people in your party. If you're bugging out with a doctor or nurse in tow, you're going to want different items in your first aid kit than you'd want if you were bugging out with a bunch of average Joes.

Take into consideration the injuries and illnesses you're likely to encounter in the area you plan on bugging out to. Consider the terrain you'll be traveling, the altitude, plants and animals you may encounter and illnesses that are common to the region.

Look at the individual medical needs of each person in your party and pack their bags accordingly. Extra medication is a must, because you can't say for sure how long you're going to be on your own. Don't forget to rotate your stock of medication so it doesn't expire and start to degrade in quality.

When it comes to first aid, your kit needs to be tailored to your individual situation. Don't buy one of those premade kits and throw it in your bag and assume you're going to be good to go. In my experience, those kits contain a lot of stuff you probably aren't going to need and not a whole of the stuff you will. Building your own kit ensures you get what you need and gives you a much better idea of what the stuff that's in your kit is there for.

That said, there are some items every bug out first aid kit should have. You need to keep in mind you're preparing for a situation in which you have no access to modern medical attention. You're going to be in the middle of nowhere and on your own should a medical emergency present itself.

Here are the items you're going to want on hand:

A quick-application tourniquet. A Combat Application Tourniquet (CAT) is your best bet for stopping bleeding from a deep wound on an arm or a leg. You need to make sure you know how to apply one ahead of time. You don't want to be attempting to apply a CAT for the first time when someone's life is on the line. Arterial wounds can cause someone to bleed out in a matter of seconds. Every second counts when you're applying a CAT. Make sure you know how to do it in advance. Practice applying it to others and have each member of your party learn to apply it to themselves. In a combat situation you may find yourself separated from the party and injured, in which case you'd have to be able to apply the CAT on your own.

A stainless steel surgical kit. While I don't recommend field surgery, you may find yourself in a situation in which being able to operate on a party member is the difference between life and death. This isn't something you can practice ahead of time, but you can read up on how to do various field procedures and at least have a rudimentary knowledge of field surgery before bugging out. Be sure to boil the instruments before using them to sterilize them. Your surgical kit should contain a scalpel or two, sharp surgical scissors, sutures and a needle. The sutures and needle should only be used if you have a trained professional on hand. You can end up sealing bacteria into a wound as opposed to helping it heal by suturing a dirty wound shut.

An anticoagulant agent. Sometimes traditional methods of stopping bleeding just won't work. When this happens, you're going to need to take more drastic action. An advanced anticoagulant device like a QuikClot Sponge can stop bleeding by speeding up the blood coagulation process and forming a stable blood clot. Be aware that anticoagulant agents should only be used in the event that traditional methods of stopping bleeding fail and there's no other choice. Read up on how and when to apply them ahead of time. There are many special considerations that must be made.

Diethyl ether and coffee filters. Diethyl ether can be sprayed on 30 or so coffee filters, which are then placed over the mouth and nose of an individual to sedate them in an emergency surgery situation. Read up on how to do this in advance because there is a very real danger of killing the person you're trying to sedate. You should never do this unless you have someone in your party who is trained in anesthesia and is able to properly administer the dosage. There is a high risk of accidentally killing the person the ether is being administered to. Never practice this one in advance. One more warning. Commercial engine starting fluids contain diethyl ether, but they aren't pure diethyl ether. Don't use them as anesthesia because there are all kinds of bad stuff in them that can cause unintended side effects.

Two books: Emergency War Surgery and Ditch Medicine. These two books will cover many of the emergency surgery and medical situations you may encounter. Read up on items likely to occur in all situations and in your particular area. Keep the books in your BOB, so you'll have them if an unusual situation should arise.

Tweezers. Get splinters out and work in areas where your chubby fingers won't fit.

Antibiotic ointment. Apply to wounds to help ward off infection and speed up healing.

Over-the counter medications. Keep a good supply of pain killers, cough medicine, allergy medications, antihistamines, anti-diarrhea medication and anything else you can think you might need on hand.

A CPR pocket resuscitator. This will allow you to easily apply CPR without mouth-to-mouth contact in the event it's required. It also prevents blood or vomit from entering the mouth of the person giving CPR from the person it's being given to.

Space blanket. Lightweight blanket that can be used to treat hypothermia and will work for extra warmth on a really cold night.

Bandages and gauze. Keep an Ace bandage, a roll of gauze, a roll of medical tape and a number of bandages of various sizes in your bag. You should also have a few butterfly bandages (or know how to make them) because they're good for cuts that aren't bad enough to really need stitches, but are deeper than what can easily be closed with a bandage.

Hand sanitization wipes or lotion. Use them to clean your hands before working on an open wound to help prevent infection.

Thermometer. See how bad a fever really is, so you know what action you need to take.

Cotton balls and Q-tips. Can be used to clean wounds and apply ointments.

Alcohol wipes. Can also be used to clean wounds and sterilize hands.

Latex gloves. Avoid touching open wounds and coming in direct contact with potentially infected blood.

A bag. You're going to want a bag to keep it all in. Don't throw each piece in your bag separately or you're going to have a tough time finding the items you need without taking everything out of your bag.

Sanitary napkins and tampons. These aren't just in there for the women in the group. They can soak up a lot of blood and work well to stop bad bloody noses. You can even tear them into little pieces and use them as tinder to start a fire.

Saline solution. Use it to irrigate wounds and to wash contaminants out of people's eyes, ears, nose and mouth.

SAM splint. A SAM splint is a handy splint that can be used to splint a fracture or as an emergency cervical collar for a neck injury. It stores away easily because it rolls up into a 5" roll.

Many of these first aid items are useless without the knowledge needed to use them. Research how to properly apply field first aid and practice the items you can safely practice.

4 Ways to Light a Fire

Figure 13: Fire. Picture by Giovanni Dall'Orto, July 2003.

Fire is basic need. It's right up there with clothing, shelter, water and food. You aren't going to last long in the woods without the ability to light a fire, especially if you have to bug out during the colder months.

There's a disturbing trend amongst budding survivalists. That trend is for them to only have one or two ways to light a fire. They throw a Zippo or butane lighter in their bag along with some fuel and feel like they're ready for anything. Sometimes they'll add a handful of waterproof matches for good measure.

Figure 14: A windproof butane lighter will be your best friend on a windy day.

You need to carry 3 lighters minimum.

If you can afford them, purchase 3 waterproof, windproof butane lighters so you can use them to light a fire when it's rainy or windy. The reason I recommend having three is because they're small and light and you should always have backup lighters. Lighters have a way of coming up missing when you need them most and you don't want to be left out in the cold. Keep one lighter in the pocket of your jeans, one in a jacket pocket and a back-up lighter and extra fuel in your BOB.

If you can't afford or otherwise don't want to spring for 3 butane lighters, buy one butane lighter and throw a couple cheaper lighters in your bag. If something happens to your good lighter, you'll have the cheap ones as backup.

You can add a film canister or two of waterproof matches to further build up your fire-building supplies. I'm not a big fan of matches because they blow out too easily, but you might as well keep a few of them on hand, too.

To be fully prepared for bugging out, you need to know how to light a fire in more ways than just using a lighter and matches. If you get separated from your bag and have to ditch it, you're going to want to be able to build a fire. It can be used for warmth, to heat food, to signal the other people in your group and as a weapon to fight off animals.

The rest of the chapter covers 3 ways you can build a fire without matches or a lighter and the supplies you're going to want to have in your bag to do so.

Friction Fires

This is the hardest method of building fires there is, but it's also the most primitive and requires the least amount of supplies from your BOB. The basic premise is if you rub two pieces of wood together for a long enough period of time the heat will build up until a glowing ember is created. The glowing ember can be moved into a tinder pile, which is a pile of highly flammable material like dryer lint, most or light wood shavings. After moving the ember into the tinder, you gently blow on it to help it light up the tender. A flame eventually arises from the tinder pile and you're in business.

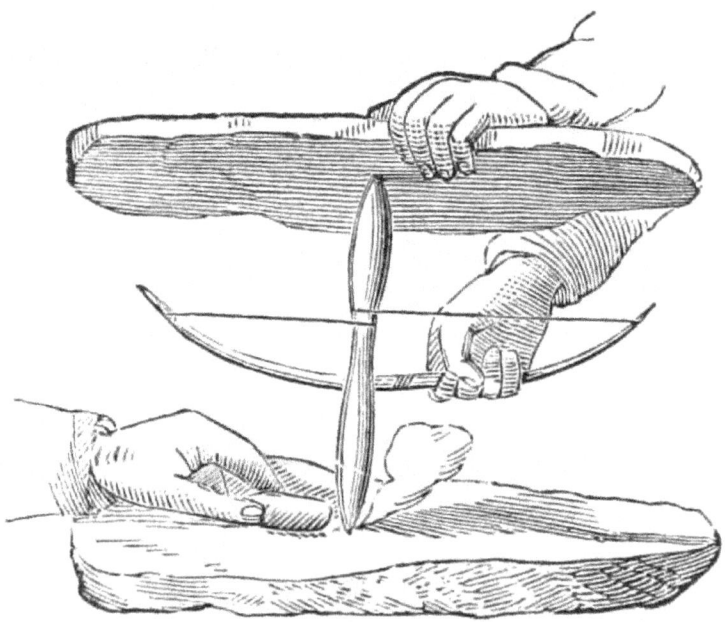

Figure 15: Bow and Drill fire starting method

The best way to light a friction fire is called the *bow and drill method*. You use a bow made from wood and a string to drill a piece of straight hardwood down into a flat piece of softwood. The friction eventually starts a fire.

The drill needs to be a piece of straight hardwood. The straighter it is, the easier it'll be to get the bow to spin it in the fire board. Sharpen the end of the bow into a point and cut a notch into the softwood fire board, so the drill will continuously rub in one place.

You need to work the bow back and forth as fast as you can. The idea is to spin the drill while using the socket to push it into down into the notch. With enough hard work and determination you'll eventually get a little ember which you can transfer into a tinder pile to light your fire.

This method only requires one tool from your bug out bag: a piece of string or cord. If you had to, you could probably use a shoelace. The tinder can be found in the wild in the form of dry moss, lichen or dried wood and bark shavings. Cattails also work well if you rub the ends between your palms and fluff them out. You can pack your own tinder if you'd like. Dryer lint is lightweight and works great as tinder.

Flint and Steel

Figure 16: This is quartzite. It can be used if you don't have a flint handy- but you've got to find a piece first.

Every good bug out bag should have a flint and steel in it. Every good survivalist should know how to use one. It's just another tool you can use to stay alive.

The way a flint and steel work is you hold the flint over a bed of tinder and run the piece of steel down the flint. A shower of sparks will rain down on your tinder pile and hopefully one of the sparks will catch. Blow gently on the ember as it forms and you'll eventually get a flame you can use to start a fire.

A regular lighter is able to be lit a thousand times if you're lucky. You can strike a good flint with steel at least a few thousand times before it's too small to use.

In order to use this method, you need to have a flint in your bug out bag. Quartzite rocks can be used if you can find them in the wild, but I wouldn't want to have to try to hunt one down while freezing to death in a driving rain. You're also going to need steel. If you don't have the steel that came as part of your flint and steel kit, you can use the backside of your hunting knife. The last thing you're going to need is tinder. You can use char cloth, which is the tinder of choice when using flint and steel because it catches quickly or you can use anything that lights up fast like dryer lint, pieces of a tampon or dried lichen or moss.

Don't just toss a flint and steel in your bag and call it a day. Practice lighting a fire with one until you're comfortable you can do it in an emergency situation.

Battery and Steel Wool

Figure 17: Keep a couple 9-colt batteries and some steel wool in your bag for yet another way you can start a fire.

This one's an easy one.

Take a wad of steel wool and lay it across both the positive and negative terminals of a 9-volt battery. The steel wool will start to glow red almost immediately. Blow on it a bit and it'll light on fire. Transfer the steel wool to your tinder pile and stoke the flame.

You can use other types of batteries as well. 9-volt batteries are easier because the positive and negative terminals are right next to one another. To use a different type of battery, twist a piece of steel wool up and hold one end on the negative terminal, then touch the other end to the positive terminal. Don't hold it on the positive terminal with your finger because it's going to heat up quickly.

Throw a couple 9-volt batteries and a few pieces of steel wool in your BOB so you'll have yet another way to light a fire.

Miscellaneous Tools and Supplies

If you're not careful, your bug out bag can start looking like a large tool chest. Even more importantly, it's going to feel like you're lugging a tool chest around on your back. You're going to want some tools to make life easier, but have to be able to decide what you have to have and what can be left behind in the name of lightening your load.

You're going to want the following tools:

Multi-tool. When it comes to tools, your best bet is going to be to buy tools able to function well in more than one capacity. You don't want to carry individual Phillips head screwdrivers, flat head screwdrivers and pliers. Instead, go with a multi-tool that contains all of them in one small package.

The SOG PowerAssist is one of the best survival multi-tools on the market. It contains the following tools:

- Pliers.
- Wire cutters.
- Cap crimper.
- A knife blade.
- A serrated knife blade.
- Phillips head and flathead screwdrivers.
- Can opener.
- Bottle opener.
- Ruler.
- A 3-sided file.
- An awl.
- V-cutter.

All of the tools are common tools except for the V-cutter. This tool contains a blade at the base of a V-shaped piece of metal. It works great for cutting seatbelts if you or someone in your party is trapped in a vehicle.

If you're looking for the most bang for your buck, the Leatherman Charge TTi is a good choice. It's got 19 tools packed into it. The SOG and the Leatherman both sell for around $120, so it's up to you to decide which is the better tool for your bag.

A radio. You're going to want a radio in your bag, so you can try to pick up bits and pieces of information about what's happening to civilization. If you bug out without a radio, you'll never know when it's safe to come back. Battery-operated radios aren't the best bet because batteries tend to lose power when they're stored for long periods of time. Get the smallest hand-crank or solar-powered AM-FM radio you can afford. You'll be able to use it to pick up radio signals so you can find out when the zombie invasion has been put to rest.

Tape. A roll of duct tape and a couple rolls of electrical tape will give you the ability to repair almost anything that breaks. Tape can also be used to lash things together. When I worked in the field, some of my tools were more tape than they were tool by the time I got back to society.

Toilet paper. This one's up to you. If you want to wipe your butt with leaves, go for it. If not, you're going to need some toilet paper. Make sure you know what's safe to wipe with and what isn't or you could be in for a world of hurt.

Flashlight and batteries. Invest in a good LED flashlight. Some of the better lights last as long as 40 hours on a single pair of AA batteries. Bring an extra bulb, too, just in case.

Hatchet. A hatchet is another tool that serves multiple purposes. It can be used to cut down trees, chop wood, cut tough meat and can be used as a weapon if the need arises. You can flip it over and use the backside of it as a hammer, so you won't have to carry a regular claw-type hammer with you.

Machete. Depending on the type of terrain you're going to be traversing, a machete may be an essential tool. If the area you're bugging out to has dense undergrowth or is a thick jungle, you're going to want a machete. A machete can also be used as a weapon.

Rope. You're going to want to have rope with you. You can use it for lashing things together and can secure yourself if you end up having to climb rocks or steep terrain. If you plan on using your rope to climb, you're going to want something strong enough to support your weight if you fall. This means going heavier with the rope. If not, 550 Paracord is light and will do the trick for the rest of your needs.

A tarp. Get a silicon-coated nylon tarp. They're expensive, but light enough to make the investment worth your while. Equinox and Integral Designs both sell tarps that can be used as ponchos on rainy days. This will eliminate the need for bulky raingear.

Sunscreen. If you or anyone in your party burns easily, you're going to want to bring along sunscreen. A party member with a bad sunburn is going to slow you down quite a bit.

Zip ties. Pack zip ties of various lengths into your BOB. You can use them to lash things together and they'll work as handcuffs if the need arises.

2 compasses. A compass will help you find your way to wherever it is you're headed. Bring along an extra in case the first one breaks. You don't want to get stranded in the middle of nowhere without a compass. Don't make the mistake of assuming GPS will work. GPS systems may go down in a big enough emergency. Practice navigating with a compass until you can get to your destination using one.

A map. Even the best of us get lost from time to time. You can use a terrain map to gain your bearings. You can also use a map to locate areas that might potentially hold water. Keep a map in your bug out bag to ensure you arrive safely at your destination.

Wire saw. A wire saw is a piece of rough wire connected to two rings. It can be used to cut through wood, metal, plastic or bone with ease. It's a lot more compact than trying to carry a regular saw. If you think you might end up using it a lot, bring an extra.

Small sewing kit. A big hole in your pants or shirt can make life uncomfortable. A small sewing kit will allow you to patch the hole up and go back to being somewhat more comfortable.

Folding shovel. You never know when you're going to need to dig and a folding shovel will make short work of most digging tasks that may arise. If your bag is getting too heavy and you don't want the added weight of a bigger shovel, you might want to consider at least throwing a spade in there. Digging with sticks and your hands is no fun.

Prepaid cell phone. Leave the phone off, but make sure it's charged. You can extend the life of the battery by charging it and removing it from phone. At some point you're going to want to come back from your bug out location and you're going to need to try to get in touch with family, friends or the authorities. There may not be a reception at your bug out spot, but there might be as you get closer to civilization on your way back. Keep a list of contact numbers with the phone.

You may have some special needs based on where you're bugging out to and who you have in your party. Carefully consider where you're planning on going and what you might need while you're out there. If you're going somewhere that gets a lot of snowfall, snowshoes and poles are probably going to be a necessity. If you have a baby or toddler, you might need items like diapers (cloth ones work best because they can be washed and reused), formula and a couple pacifiers. Assess the location season-by-season and your party person-by-person to ensure you're bringing everything you need.

Survival Knife

Figure 18: This is a knife.

You're going to need a good knife to cut stuff with.

Don't go too cheap on your survival knife. I can't stress this enough. You're going to rely on your knife a lot. You don't want it to fail when you need it most.

Get a *full-tang* knife. Full-tang means the blade extends through the handle. Forget about any knife that has a hollow storage compartment in the handle because they aren't full-tang knives and should be avoided. This weakens the knife and throws off the balance.

Stainless steel is probably your best bet as far as blade material goes, but there are good carbon steel knives on the market, too. Stainless steel lasts forever and a day and is able to take a beating. Stainless steel blades will eventually begin to discolor and rust if they aren't cleaned and cared for properly, but it takes a long time. Definitely longer than 72 hours. Carbon steel, on the other hand, isn't as durable and needs to be kept out of the elements, but it's strong and able to hold an edge better. It's up to you to decide which blade type is the better choice for your personal needs.

You want a knife that's at least 6 inches long. 9 to 10 inches is even better. Get any bigger than that and you're going to have a tough time using your knife for precision cutting tasks like slicing food or fileting fish. Avoid knives with a lot of flex in the blade. You want something sturdy that can take some abuse.

The handle should feel good in your hands and be non-slip. Look for a handle that has a solid, flat butt. You can use it to hammer on stuff when the need arises.

Folding blade knives are similar to pocket knives in that they fold up so they can be stored away. You can carry a pocketknife if you want, but don't buy a folding blade survival knife. You're going to use it for hacking and chopping tasks and the point at which it folds is a possible weak point.

The sheath is what attaches your knife to your body. You're better off wearing your knife than you are throwing it in your bag. Get a sheath with a belt loop or an attachment you can use to strap it to your arm or leg.

Figure 19: The strong, the proud, the Marines.

You don't want to make the wrong choice when it comes time to buy your survival knife. I'm old school and prefer a good old fashioned KA-BAR USMC Utility Knife. They've been around since WWII and are probably the most used utility knife on the planet—and for good reason. They're durable, hold an edge well and are easy to sharpen when they start to go dull. You could sharpen one with a smooth stone if you had to.

Get a good knife and learn how to use, sharpen and wear it. You might even want to learn how to properly use it in a combat situation. You wouldn't be the first person who fought off an attacker with a KA-BAR.

Packing Heat: Protect Yourself

Figure 20: Just how much heat you pack is up to you.

The weapon(s) you bring along when you bug out should be appropriate to the bug out situation.

If you're bugging out because a hurricane is headed your way and you need to head to the nearest shelter, arriving there armed to the teeth is a good way to get arrested—or worse. On the other hand, if you've just got word the U.S. has been invaded by China and Russia and a brain-sucking alien zombie horde is headed your way, you're going to want some firepower.

When it comes to weapons, I'm of the opinion it's better to have them and not need them than to need them and not have them. Keep them by your BOB and you can make the determination as to whether you're going to need them or not when you bug out.

At the bare minimum you should have a pistol and a rifle, with enough ammo to last you three days. If you have more than one person capable of carrying a weapon, add a shotgun into the mix, too. Carrying a shotgun, handgun and rifle covers near, far and mid-range combat and gives you the means to kill all types of game animal.

Ammo is heavy, so you're not going to want to pack more than 4 to 6 magazines per weapon. Instead of storing ammo in the box, get extra magazines and store the ammo in the magazine. That way if there's an active shooter situation, you don't have to take time to reload clips. You have them loaded and ready to go. You can stockpile more ammo at your bug out location. Remember, the whole idea of a bug out bag is for it to last you 72 hours so you can get to your bug out location, not so you can fight a month-long battle against the enemy.

It's important to weigh the value of protecting yourself against the laws of the land.

You probably aren't going to want to pack heavy heat in the city when there's still a police presence enforcing local laws. On the other hand, a concealed handgun will allow you to discreetly protect yourself until you can get out of town. If you plan on *bugging in*, which means staying in your home or current location and waiting things out, all bets are off. You can have as much firepower in your home as you feel comfortable with.

If you have the ability to get a concealed carry permit in your jurisdiction, do it. This will allow you to carry a concealed handgun on your person wherever you go. Make sure you know your local laws because there are still a limited number of places you can't carry. Not only will this allow you to legally carry a gun in the city in a bug out situation, it'll allow you to protect yourself and your family in everyday life. Also be aware that all of your rights up to and including your right to carry concealed may be suspended in the event of an emergency.

Figure 21: The Springfield 1911 is a great choice for self-defense.

A good pistol will cover you for both mid-range and close-quarters combat situations, but only if you're properly prepared. Keep clips at the ready in their own pocket in your BOB, so you can get to them when you need them. You may want to carry a couple extra clips on your person as well. That way, if you get separated from your bag, you'll still have some firepower at your disposal.

You're going to want to practice drawing your weapon and shooting while on the move. Combat situations rarely allow for you to stand still and carefully take aim at your adversary. You need to be able to shoot and hit a target while moving. Practice shooting torso targets in their center of mass. The torso is the easiest place to hit because there's more room for variance in your aim. If you miss and hit a limb, you're still going to put a world of hurt on your target.

Where you store your gun should depend on the situation. If you're in a situation where combat is likely, you want to keep it on your person, either in a holster that's visible or one that's concealed away out of sight. If you're concerned about the law, you might be better off hiding your gun out of sight or in your bag where it isn't going to attract unwanted attention. An exposed weapon will open you up to all sorts of harassment.

You've got some choices to make when it comes to what type of pistol you want to carry.

The first choice is the caliber. Since the gun may have to be used to defend yourself, you're going to want something with some stopping power. That means you need to carry a 9mm weapon at a bare minimum. Carry something smaller than that and you're just inviting trouble. Could you kill someone with a smaller caliber? Sure, but it's a lot easier to stop someone with a .40 or a .45.

It helps to keep in mind why you're carrying the weapon. You want to be able to protect yourself and your party members. Shooting someone with a .22 in the arm or shoulder probably isn't going to stop them in the heat of battle. On the other hand, if you hit someone with a .45 in the arm or shoulder, there's going to be a significant amount of damage. They may not die, but they'll be out of the battle, which is all you're really worried about.

You're also going to have to decide between getting a revolver or a semi-automatic. While there's something to be said about carrying a Dirty Harry-sized revolver on your hip, I think the semi-automatic wins hands-down in a bug out situation. It's easier to reload as long as you're carrying extra clips and has a larger round capacity, which means you won't have to reload as often.

Each person in your party capable of carrying a handgun should carry one. You can never have too many people with guns in a combat situation.

Rifle

Figure 22: An AR or AK platform rifle is a good choice when it comes to bugging out.

In a truly lawless world, you're going to want to have a rifle you can defend yourself with. An AR-platform rifle is a good choice for self-defense.

You're going to want your rifle set up for self-defense, while still retaining the ability to hunt game animals. When it comes to bugging out, you can cover all bases by buying a scope and adding sights that attach to the side of your gun. For long distances, you can use the scope. Up close, you can turn the gun sideways and use the sights.

When it comes to aiming at your target, the red and green dot scopes and lasers are nice, but what are you going to do if you have to bug out for longer than 72-hours and your batteries die? A good old fashioned scope and reticle sights are a better option because you don't need batteries.

The caliber of rifle you carry is up to you. You can go with the go-to military caliber of 5.56 X 45 mm NATO round. This chamber can also fire .223 rounds. If you end up having to scavenge homes and bodies for ammo, this is going to be one of the easier rounds to find. It's also going to be one of the first to run out when people start stockpiling ammo, so stock up now and make sure you're prepared. A .223 can hit targets up 600 yards out, but the effectiveness of taking down a target at that range is in question.

The 5.56 X 45 mm NATO round was designed to take targets down and wound them instead of killing them. This is the perfect round for war because instead of killing a target outright, it consumes enemy resources by requiring medical care for wounded combatants. In a bug out situation, you might decide you want more power. If you find yourself having to hunt big game animals like deer and moose, you don't want to injure them with a .223 round. You want to take them down.

If you want a rifle with more stopping power, go with the 7.62 X 51mm NATO chambered AR-10 rifle. The commercial version of this round is the .308. These rounds hit harder than the .223 and are more likely to kill, as opposed to simply putting down a target. They're good for both combat and killing game animals. The trade-off is the bullets are heavier and you're less likely to find .308 ammo in the field.

In a situation where you don't want to draw unnecessary attention to yourself, you may not want to carry an assault weapon. A group of people bugging out that are all carrying assault weapons is going to cause people to take notice. If you want to stay low-key, regular rifles may be a better choice. A 30-.06 rifle hits hard and can take down pretty much anything you decide to shoot it at.

If you have youth in your group who are responsible enough to carry a firearm, you can equip them with .22 caliber rifles. The ammo is light and the guns can be used to shoot small game animals. You'll be able to conserve the ammo in your defense weapons for when you really need it.

Shotgun

Figure 23: Carry a shotgun for close-quarters combat and to kill small game animals and birds.

If you have the ability to carry multiple weapons, you're going to want a shotgun. A good rifle and a pistol should be your first priority, with a shotgun rounding out your weapons cache.

A 12-gauge shotgun is a great weapon for close-quarter combat. It has good take-down power at short distances and the spread of the pellets means you don't have to have the greatest aim. Just point the end of the gun in the direction of the person you want to take down and fire away. A shotgun can be indispensable when it comes to getting out of town in a truly lawless situation.

Once you make it out of town, close quarters combat becomes less likely and the shotgun becomes a less-valuable weapon. It can be used to kill small game animals and birds, but the likelihood of getting close enough to an enemy combatant in the wilderness to use a shotgun is unlikely for all but the stealthiest of individuals.

Don't Forget Fido

Figure 24: You weren't thinking of leaving me behind, were you?

Planning on bringing a beloved family pet with you? Make sure you pack a bag for your pet, too.

I wouldn't recommend bringing pets other than dogs with you on the trail, but if you plan on bugging out via vehicle, you can get away with bringing other types of animals. No matter what type of pet you're bringing along, you're going to need supplies.

The good thing about most dogs is they can carry their own bags when you bug out. There are special bags for dogs that look like miniature versions of saddle bags. These bags can be packed with the supplies your dog needs to survive 72 hours and strapped to your dog's back when you bug out.

You're going to want to pack the following supplies for your pet:

- **Collapsible bowl for feeding.**
- **Water.**
- **Food.**
- **A jacket and boots.** Yes, seriously. Your pet will be more comfortable walking when warm and will be less likely to stop and try to slow you down. Boots will prevent them from picking up burrs and other items in their paws. If you have a dog you already take into the woods with you and it does fine, you can eliminate the jacket and boots.
- **Pet first aid kit.** You can buy a prepackaged pet first aid kit from most vets.
- **A carrier.** If you're planning on bringing animals other than a dog, you need a way to carry your pet. Look for a carrier that's lightweight and can be attached to your BOB.

Make sure you get your pet used to any clothing you plan on having it wear ahead of time. They aren't going to like wearing clothes at first and may sit down and refuse to move when you first put them on. Or they might freak out. You don't want this to happen when you're in the middle of a crisis situation. You should also practice putting the bag on your dog and having it walk around with it on.

Don't Procrastinate

Purchasing all the gear required for putting together a good bug out bag is expensive and time-consuming. It's all too easy to look at the list of stuff you need and to say it's going to have to wait because you can't afford everything.

Even if you can't afford top-notch gear, you need to put together something. If you can't afford an ultra-light backpack, use an old school backpack or a duffel bag and put the gear you have on hand in it. An old bag full of used gear is better than having nothing when it comes time to bug out.

Add stuff to your bag as you can afford it. Buying items one at a time as your finances allow gives you time to save up for the items you truly want. Buy a good bag first, and then slowly build up your stock of quality gear. Items like tents, sleeping bags, tools and weapons last a long time if properly cared for, so you're only going to have to buy them once.

Don't put off putting together a bag just because you can't afford the best of best right now.

You're going to want something to bug out with, regardless of the quality of the items you have. Put together a bag and practice using the items you have on hand until you're comfortable with them. It could mean the difference between survival and being one of the victims when and if a bug out situation presents itself.

www.ingramcontent.com/pod-product-compliance
Lightning Source LLC
Chambersburg PA
CBHW070543290526
45790CB00002B/588

* 9 7 8 1 4 8 1 1 6 5 9 0 7 *